Developing Digital Literacy

CREATING A WEBSITE

BY ANNA COLLINS

Cavendish Square

New York

Published in 2023 by Cavendish Square Publishing, LLC
29 East 21st Street New York, NY 10010

Website: cavendishsq.com

This publication represents the opinions and views of the author based on their personal experience, knowledge, and research. The information in this book serves as a general guide only. The author and publisher have used their best efforts in preparing this book and disclaim liability rising directly or indirectly from the use and application of this book.

Disclaimer: Portions of this work were originally authored by J. Poolos and published as *Designing, Building, and Maintaining Websites* (Digital and Information Literacy™). All new material this edition authored by Anna Collins.

All websites were available and accurate when this book was sent to press.

Cataloging-in-Publication Data

Names: Collins, Anna.
Title: Creating a website / Anna Collins.
Description: New York : Cavendish Square Publishing, 2023. | Series: Developing digital literacy | Includes glossary and index.
Identifiers: ISBN 9781502665669 (pbk.) | ISBN 9781502665676 (library bound) | ISBN 9781502665683 (ebook)
Subjects: LCSH: Web site development–Juvenile literature. | Web sites–Design–Juvenile literature.
Classification: LCC TK5105.888 C65 2023 | DDC 006.7–dc23

Editor: Jennifer Lombardo
Copy editor: Michele Suchomel-Casey
Designer: Deanna Paternostro

The photographs in this book are used by permission and through the courtesy of: Series background Olga Tsyvinska/Shutterstock.com; cover image Julia Tim/Shutterstock.com; cover, pp. 11, 16, 32, 39 (frame) Panuwatccn/Shutterstock.com; cover, pp. 5, 9, 15, 27, 35 (banner background) The7Dew/Shutterstock.com; p. 4 PureSolution/Shutterstock.com; pp. 6–7 REDPIXEL.PL/Shutterstock.com; p. 8 VLADGRIN/Shutterstock.com; p. 10 alexaldo/Shutterstock.com; p. 12 Stock image/Shutterstock.com; p. 14 sliplee/Shutterstock.com; p. 17 Flamingo Images/Shutterstock.com; p. 19 JanPetrskovsky/Shutterstock.com; p. 21 Akin Ozcan/Shutterstock.com; p. 23 Jozsef Bagota/Shutterstock.com; p. 24 Alexey Boldin/Shutterstock.com; p. 26 EgudinKa/Shutterstock.com; p. 29 Archive PL/Alamy Stock Photo; p. 33 McLittle Stock/Shutterstock.com; p. 34 Jiw Ingka/Shutterstock.com; p. 36 JMiks/Shutterstock.com; p. 39 PixieMe/Shutterstock.com; p. 41 (top) Chekyravaa/Shutterstock.com; p. 41 (bottom) MIND AND I/Shutterstock.com.

Some of the images in this book illustrate individuals who are models. The depictions do not imply actual situations or events.

CPSIA compliance information: Batch #CSCSQ23: For further information contact Cavendish Square Publishing LLC, New York, New York, at 1-877-980-4450.

Printed in the United States of America

Find us on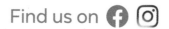

Contents

In the early days of the internet, people did not hire professional web designers. Today, however, web design is a fast-growing career field.

INTRODUCTION

In the 1990s, when the internet was first becoming widespread, a website was considered a **novelty**. Many people did not see the point in making one, and the ones that existed were often built just for fun by people with a lot of knowledge about how this new technology worked.

Today, all of this has changed. Now, it is rare for a business not to have a website. In fact, most people agree that a website—or at the very least, a presence on social media—is essential for businesses as well as for people who are looking for work. Tools offered by businesses such as Squarespace and Wix make it easy for anyone to make a basic website, but for more advanced or unique sites, people generally hire professionals called web developers.

Web developers must think carefully about what they hope to accomplish when developing a site. A website needs to look good, work well, and be easy to use. Planning helps web developers meet all of these goals. Web developers also need to have a certain set of skills. For example, they should have a good eye for graphic design,

WEB DEVELOPERS HAVE TO UNDERSTAND BOTH CODING AND GRAPHIC DESIGN.

and they absolutely need to understand how to code, as this is what makes the website actually work. Web developers generally need to know several programming languages to make quick, **efficient** websites. They also need to know how to troubleshoot, which means fixing both predictable problems and unexpected ones that may arise.

For a web developer, learning is not finished when they graduate from school because technology is always changing. To make websites that look up to date, they need to read about the latest advancements and learn when and how to put them to use. However, personal websites do not need to be as impressive as the ones for businesses. This means anyone can either learn basic coding or use a pre-set **template** to make a website about any topic they want. The internet is full of both simple and complex websites, and learning the basics of web design, or the creation of a website, is the foundation of learning how to make both kinds.

WEBSITES ARE JUST ONE WAY PEOPLE
CAN USE THE INTERNET TO CONNECT
WITH ONE ANOTHER. THEY'RE A GREAT
WAY TO GIVE PEOPLE INFORMATION.

CHAPTER ONE

WEB BASICS

Websites are such a common part of our lives that people sometimes forget they have not been around for very long. Computers were not able to share information with each other until the 1960s, when the U.S. Department of Defense (DoD) began to work on creating a network of computers. Their work took many years. Finally, in 1991, the World Wide Web—which is what we use to access the internet—went live to the public for the first time.

Today, there are websites for just about everything. People use them to share information through text, pictures, video, audio, and more. News organizations publish stories and videos online, allowing more people than ever to stay up to date on what is happening around the world. Universities offer remote classes so students can learn from home. Businesses of all kinds sell their products and services online. Individuals share their ideas on blogs, create communities, and share news and media either on websites they have made themselves or through social media websites such as Facebook, Twitter, and Instagram. A person who has any kind of question can pull up Google and try to find the answer, and coding is taught in schools around the world.

```
<!DOCTYPE html>
2 ▼ <html lang="en">
3 ▼     <head>
4           <meta charset="utf-8">
5           <meta name="viewport" content="width=device-width, initial-scale=1">
6           <title>Lorem Ipsum</title>
7           <link rel="stylesheet" href="style.css">
8           <link href="https://fonts.googleapis.com/css2?family=Kaushan+Script&family=Montserrat:300i,wght@400;700&"
            rel="stylesheet">
9           <link rel="stylesheet"
            href="https://use.fontawesome.com/releases/v5.7.2/css
            integrity="sha384-
            fnm0CqbTlWIlj8LyTjo7mOUStjsKC4pOpQbqyi7RrhN7udi9R
            crossorigin="anonymous">
            </head>
10
11 ▼ <body>
12 ▼     <div class="header" id="header">
13 ▼         <div class="container">
14 ▼             <div class="header-inner">
15                  <div class="logo">Lorem Ipsum</di
16 ▼                 <nav class="nav">
                        <a class="nav-link active" h
                        <a class="nav-link" href="
                        <a class="nav-link" hre
                            ="nav-link" hr
```

CODE SUCH AS THIS IS WHAT MAKES WEBSITES WORK.

UNDERSTANDING THE LANGUAGE

The internet is a worldwide system of computer networks through which data travels. The web can be thought of as the collection of websites that exist on the internet. The three parts that allow the web to function are the browser, the page, and the server.

EARLY CODING

In the 1990s, a web-hosting service called GeoCities allowed users to create their own web pages about anything they wanted. To make one, users needed a good knowledge of HTML (hypertext markup language). In the early 2000s, the first social media websites started appearing. One of these, MySpace, was similar to what Facebook is now. However, MySpace allowed users to change the HTML of their page to make it very personal. Unlike GeoCities, a MySpace page was free, which made basic coding accessible to everyone. Because the internet was so new, coding was not yet being taught in schools, so this was how many young people learned about it at the time.

Due to an initial mistake, MySpace let people change just about everything—their cursor, font color, background image, and much more—by giving them access to their page's HTML. Users loved it, so the developers kept the mistake as a permanent part of the site, even though it caused security problems. While some people simply copied and pasted changes other users had made, many people actually taught themselves coding basics by changing things until they figured out how the process worked. MySpace made a whole generation interested in the possibilities of coding.

A web browser, such as Mozilla Firefox or Google Chrome, is a software application used to retrieve web pages from web servers and to convert them from HTML to a form a user can easily read. Browsers are installed on a user's digital devices.

An HTML document is a document that is displayed by a web browser. Made up of text, HTML documents include both content and directions that tell the browser how to display the content. For example, the actual web page the user views may display the word "Hello." The HTML document contains this content (the word "Hello") and guidelines for its display—such as it being centered on the page and in 12-point type.

A web server is the software that delivers (or serves) web pages when someone requests them as well as the computers that run these programs. The computers known as servers are not like everyday, personal computers. Instead, they are generally large pieces of hardware that are kept in special climate-controlled rooms, due to the large amounts of heat they put out.

COMPUTER SERVERS SUCH AS THIS ONE ARE LARGE PIECES OF EQUIPMENT.

PROGRAMMING LANGUAGES

Designing a website requires understanding how these three parts work together to make the internet we access every day. Although certain services make publishing a website easier than ever, a basic knowledge of how to use HTML code to change what is displayed on the website is helpful.

When a person creates a web page in an HTML editor, they put the HTML code in brackets called tags on either side of the word. For example, this is how someone would make a word bold using HTLM code. The tags do not display on the web page. Only the words display, along with the formatting—in this case, the bold typeface.

HTML is the building block for web page authoring, but there are other programming languages that can tell the browser how to display a web page. These include CSS, Flash, Javascript, and XML. These languages are more advanced and powerful than HTML, and they allow knowledgeable web page authors to build fast, user-friendly websites.

Think About It

1. Why do you think people were excited about being able to change the HTML on their MySpace page?
2. Why do you think the internet was such an important invention?
3. How does knowing HTML help a person build a better website?

STARTING WITH A
PLAN CAN SAVE
A WEB DESIGNER
HOURS OF WORK.

CHAPTER TWO

DESIGN AND PLANNING

A lot of work goes into designing a website. As making a website has gotten easier over the years, the amount of information available online has exploded—and not all of it is accurate. The way a website looks is generally a person's first clue about whether or not a website is legitimate, or accurate, so it needs to look professional. This requires careful planning. Furthermore, planning the layout can ensure that the website is easy to use. Most people will not spend a lot of time trying to figure out how to access what they need on a website, so they will leave if it is not easy to use.

FIGURING OUT THE PURPOSE

Every website begins with a goal. The goal will determine the direction that the web design takes. Thinking about this purpose lets the web designer start big and then work their way down to the smaller details.

If the intention is to deliver information about horses, for instance, the first thing to consider is exactly what kind of information about horses the website will cover. The second is to think about how that information will be displayed. Will the site have only text, or will it also have photos and videos?

A site that is intended to sell books will be designed differently. The person designing the site would want it to display the books so

WHY MAKE A WEBSITE?

In 2019, Jessica Stevenson decided to start a candy store called Hello, Sweets! Candy and Pop Shop. She did not believe she needed a website because her store was small and local to Tonawanda, New York. She said, "We made a basic website with just our name and address on it shortly after we opened, but it wasn't until the COVID-19 pandemic that we felt like we needed a website that was also an online store. That helped us sell online so we could stay in business when people were trying to stay home."

Because business was slow but steady, Jessica did not worry too much about whether the website's **inventory** matched what was in the store. However, when the store unexpectedly went viral on TikTok in early 2021, TikTok users bought everything that was listed on the site—some of which had already sold out in the physical store. Jessica and her husband, Tyler, quickly realized that with the increase in business, they would need to put more effort into the website. Now, they keep a separate online inventory and fill orders for people in the United States and Canada. They do about six times as much business online as they do in the store. Tyler said, "Most people shop online, but they also like to support small, local businesses. If a small business has a website, customers can do both."

potential buyers can easily view all the different options. Clicking on a book could bring users to a different page that explains what the book is about, what it costs, and how to buy it. Splitting information into separate parts of the website makes it easier for people to see exactly what they want. Putting all of this information on the main page makes it too cluttered and hard to read. For websites, sometimes less is more.

TARGETING AN AUDIENCE

After the web designer has determined the website's basic goals and needs, it is time to consider the needs of the site's audience. These are the people the creator wants to attract to the website. Most members of the audience will have something in common. In the examples above, they all may be interested in horses or in buying books.

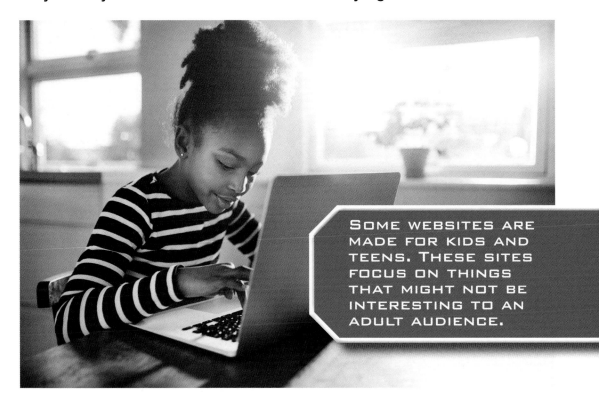

SOME WEBSITES ARE MADE FOR KIDS AND TEENS. THESE SITES FOCUS ON THINGS THAT MIGHT NOT BE INTERESTING TO AN ADULT AUDIENCE.

Knowing their audience can allow a designer to focus the site's content on what will appeal to its visitors. Some websites are aimed at beginners, while others are aimed at experts. For example, there are websites that explain science concepts to people who do not understand much about them, and there are other websites that are made specifically for scientists. A teenager who visits the second page might not understand any of it, and a scientist who visits the first page might be bored by reading things they already know. It is OK not to appeal to every single person. In fact, it is considered a good thing because it allows a website to focus on meeting a specific need instead of trying to fit too much unnecessary information on a page. To figure out exactly what information the website will focus on, it can be very helpful to make a list of all the bits of data, topics, and subtopics it should cover. Organizing these can come later, but deciding on the level of detail the site will provide is an important first step.

Once the site's content has been determined, it's time to decide how best to deliver the information to the audience. There are many options for presenting content on the web. Each one has its benefits and drawbacks. For example, a text-only website is easy to make and can deliver a lot of information at once, but it is not very eye-catching, so visitors may lose interest. Adding photos can address this problem and can also help illustrate concepts that are hard to describe in text, but an image-heavy website loads more slowly.

MAKING THE LAYOUT

A website's design and construction bring together three different aspects: how it is structured, how its various pages are laid out, and how users can navigate around it. Designers use these three elements to make sure information is easy to find on their site. This is especially important for business websites. People who have trouble navigating around a site are not likely to stick around long enough to buy something.

Website users want to access content or accomplish a goal without any hassle. A site fails in its mission if users get lost or unnecessarily

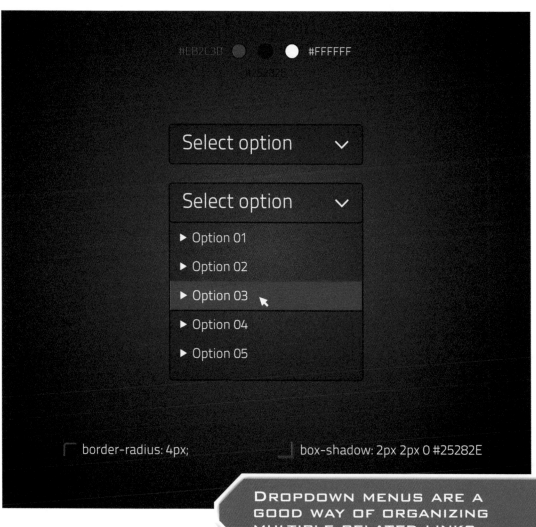

DROPDOWN MENUS ARE A GOOD WAY OF ORGANIZING MULTIPLE RELATED LINKS.

distracted, or cannot figure out which link best serves their needs. Of course, this means all the links need to be easy to find and properly labeled. Many websites use a dropdown menu that is labeled either with the word "menu" or with a symbol made up of three horizontal lines. Some **embed** links into the text; these are easy to see because they are often underlined and the font is often in a different color.

If a website has a lot of information to share, a designer may choose to use more dropdown menus. To use the bookstore website as an example again, the site may have menus at the top of the page with labels such as "comic books," "fiction," "nonfiction," and "journals." Each dropdown menu may then be further divided. For example, clicking on "comic books" might reveal more links such as "DC," "Marvel," and "Image." Clicking on each of those will take the user to comic books that fit into those categories. If there are more than a few links, the designer may decide instead to make the "comic books" link take the user to a completely different page that is easier to navigate.

LOOKING GOOD

Making a website easy to use is important, but it is equally important to make it look good so it is easy to read and navigate. Furthermore, people are more likely to trust websites that are nicely designed. In the 1990s, having a website at all was seen as a mark of legitimacy. However, when some people started hiring professional graphic designers to create their websites, people started to see the old designs as ugly. A similar thing happens with physical stores. Would you be more likely to trust a shop that had a professional-looking sign, or one that had a sign made out of cardboard and markers?

Businesses often hire professional graphic designers to make their websites because they have studied the way things catch people's eyes. They use visual **hierarchy** to direct a user's eye to certain parts of the website first. For example, a title in large letters catches the eye first. Bright colors also catch the eye sooner than muted colors. However, bright colors can be difficult to look at for a long time, so it is best to use them only for things the designer wants their audience to look at first. On a website where visual hierarchy has not been used, visitors often find it difficult to figure out where to look first, which can be overwhelming and may make them leave the page.

VISUAL HIERARCHY WORKS LIKE A HIGHLIGHTER TO DIRECT PEOPLE'S EYES NATURALLY TO CERTAIN PLACES. IF THE ENTIRE PAGE IS HIGHLIGHTED, IT DOES NOT WORK THE SAME WAY. THIS IS WHY DESIGNERS NEED TO UNDERSTAND WHEN AND WHERE TO USE CERTAIN FEATURES.

In the early days of website creation, people often used many elements, such as text art, detailed backgrounds, and animations. These could be fun to look at, but they generally made a site hard to read. When trying to get information across, less is more. Backgrounds should be neutral colors, not too bright or patterned. Text should be in a font and color that is easy to read, and it should be consistent throughout. A design scheme should also be consistent. Banners, backgrounds, colors, fonts, and navigation buttons should have a similar appearance, including matching colors, from page to page. This way, the visitor can feel comfortable with the design and focus on the content.

Website elements are generally arranged in columns on the page. The number of columns depends on the style of website. A blog, or online journal, will often only have one column, while a news website may have three or four. Many websites also arrange their information in an F-shaped pattern. This means the information they want the user to see first is on the top left, moving toward the right. The second-most important information will be on the left below it, again moving toward the right, and so on. This is done because people read English from left to right. Think about how you start reading a page in a book. You start at the top left, move to the right, then move down to the next line. Well-designed websites mimic this reading style in their overall layout.

When using images on a website, it is important to consider how many images will be loaded, as well as their size. Images are loaded from the server and displayed in the browser, just like text, but they take longer than text to load, especially if they are large. Anyone designing a site should be careful not to use too many images on each page

THIS WEBSITE IS AN EXAMPLE OF THE F-SHAPED LAYOUT. THE EYE IS DRAWN FIRST TO THE HEADLINE AT THE TOP, THEN DOWN AND ACROSS THE NAVIGATION BAR, THEN FURTHER DOWN AND ACROSS THE FOLLOWING ROWS.

and to take care with the image size. Once an image is loaded, it is stored in the browser's **cache**. An image can be loaded from the cache more quickly than it can be loaded from the server. Website developers can take advantage of this by using the same image on several pages to reduce loading time. Website visitors who have newer computers and fast internet connections will likely not have a problem loading most websites, but web developers also need to think about people who do not have access to these things. Acceptable image formats for use on a website include GIF (graphics interchange format), JPEG (joint photographic experts group format), and PNG (portable network graphic). GIF files are good for line-art illustrations, like drawings. They are also used to animate a series of photos, like a flipbook. This is

WEB DESIGNERS NEED TO MAKE SURE A WEBSITE LOOKS GOOD NO MATTER WHAT DEVICE SOMEONE IS VIEWING IT ON.

because unlike most other file formats, GIF can hold multiple pictures at once. JPEG files are good for photographs. PNG files are especially popular with web designers because they can store more detail than GIFs or JPEGs. In fact, PNG was designed to be used online, so this type of file is used most often. Images must also be sized to fit in the layout and to load quickly. If an image is too large or if the designer does not specify its dimensions, the browser can take longer to load it. This is the downside of PNG files: Because they are more detailed, they are also larger.

Web developers also need to think about how their website will look on different devices. Around 2008, smartphones started to become advanced enough to load websites. However, people were still designing websites only for computers, so the sites were often difficult to read on phones. Today, the majority of users access the internet mainly or solely from their phones, so designers need to make sure their website looks good on mobile devices as well as on laptop and desktop computers.

Think About It

1. If most websites use the same visual hierarchy, why don't they all look exactly the same?
2. What are some other ways designers can use visual hierarchy to direct a user's eye?
3. What are some differences between a good layout on a computer and a good layout on a phone?

```
<html>
 <head>

 </head>
 <body>

 </body>
</html>
```

Chapter THREE

WEBSITE CONSTRUCTION

After the purpose and design are planned out, it is time to build the website. The first part of this process is choosing a program to build the site. People who want to code all of their own HTML need an HTML editing program, such as Adobe Dreamweaver. Those who want the basics done for them but still want to be able to customize things can choose from a number of websites. One popular choice is WordPress. In fact, almost half of all websites are built with this site. It is especially good for people who know how to use CSS (Cascading Style Sheets) to customize their website. While HTML builds the actual site, CSS allows people to change the way the site looks. It can be used to determine things such as fonts, colors, and the placement of images and text. Without CSS, a website will work, but it will look no different than a Microsoft Word document with links in it.

For people who want to publish a website but do not know much about coding, there are easy-to-use websites that also function as hosts. These hosts give people a place on the internet to display their own website. Many sites charge money to host a website, but some, such as Wix and Squarespace, offer basic services for free.

10 Most Popular Website Builders in 2022

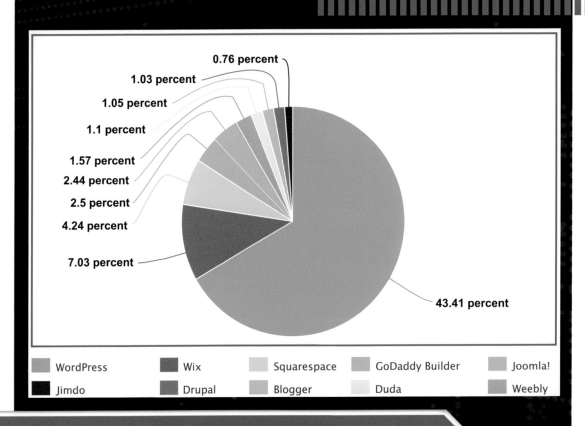

- 0.76 percent
- 1.03 percent
- 1.05 percent
- 1.1 percent
- 1.57 percent
- 2.44 percent
- 2.5 percent
- 4.24 percent
- 7.03 percent
- 43.41 percent

WordPress ■ Wix ■ Squarespace ■ GoDaddy Builder ■ Joomla!

Jimdo ■ Drupal ■ Blogger ■ Duda ■ Weebly

WORDPRESS IS BY FAR THE MOST POPULAR WEBSITE BUILDER, ACCORDING TO THIS INFORMATION FROM FIRSTSITEGUIDE.

A DEVELOPER'S TOOLBOX

Developers build websites using software applications called tools. These tools make the job of building the website easier and faster. When it comes to building a basic website, only a few tools are needed.

If a developer chooses to code their own website, they need an HTML editor. These programs allow designers to input HTML code. Many HTML editors also include features that let them use dropdown menus to generate the code. One of the big advantages of an HTML editor is that a user can use the menus to accomplish a task and then view the code the editor generates. This is a great way to learn how to code HTML. Some hosting sites allow subscribers to use their HTML editors. One of the most popular HTML editors is Adobe Dreamweaver.

IF COMPUTER ACCESS IS LIMITED, CODING CAN BE DONE ON PAPER. SHOWN HERE IS MARGARET HAMILTON, A NASA SCIENTIST, STANDING NEXT TO A STACK OF CODE THAT WAS WRITTEN BY HAND AND PUT INTO THE COMPUTER LATER.

Graphics programs are also important tools in web design. They are used to change and move images, such as photographs. For example, a graphics program can be used to change the size of an image so it fits on a web page or crop images to improve the way they look with the other elements on the page. Adobe Photoshop is by far the most popular graphics program, but it is fairly expensive. Free ones that also allow for the creation of web elements include Vectr and SVG-edit.

In addition to graphics editors, illustration programs let people make line drawings and even add colors and patterns to a website. Some people use illustration programs to make cartoons for their sites or buttons for their navigation menus. Again, Adobe is the most popular here, with its Illustrator program. However, there are many options developers can shop around for.

HTML STANDARDS

Knowing HTML is important for a designer who wants to build a site from the ground up. HTML is a programming language, and like a spoken language, it has rules. If someone codes their website incorrectly, it will not work. Furthermore, the site needs to be coded according to the rules created by the World Wide Web Consortium (W3C), which is the group that creates web standards. Code that follows these standards will work consistently across various browsers and operating systems.

W3C standards require certain elements on each page. For instance, each page must begin and end with the <html> tag. Each must have a heading as well. A basic page in HTML looks something like this:

```
<html>
<head>
<title>The Title of the Page Goes Here</title>
</head>
<body>
All text, images, and other elements go here.
</body>
</html>
```

The tags, such as <title> and </title>, surround the content and tell the browser how to display it on the screen. The smallest error—for example, not including the slash before the word in the end tag—means the code will not work. There are many different tags available, and they are used for all sorts of purposes, including changing the size and color of text, putting space between paragraphs, and locating elements on a page. Users can see the code on any web page by performing specific actions, depending on the computer and web browser they are using. They cannot change the code, but they can see exactly what makes the page work.

Today, most developers use CSS to define the way the HTML is displayed on the page. The style sheet is a separate file containing only tags and instructions for display. Each web page refers to this file for display instructions. The advantage of CSS is that a developer can change any style on the website just by editing the style sheet, rather than by editing the HTML of each page of the site.

NAVIGATING THE WEBSITE

Another important design consideration in the construction of a website is the navigation menu. Navigation menus contain the links a visitor clicks on to move from one page to another. Because navigation menus are heavily used by visitors to a website, they need to be user-friendly. Someone who has trouble figuring out how to get from one page to another will not stay on the site long. One basic rule is that the navigation menu should display in the same place on every page of the site. This way, it is always easy for the user to find.

Navigation menus can be simple or **dynamic**. A simple navigation menu is just a list of links. A dynamic navigation menu changes when the visitor hovers over it. For example, the navigation menu may include dropdown menus. Another option for a dynamic navigation menu is to make the links change color or turn bold when someone hovers over them.

WHAT ARE WIDGETS?

A widget is a device that is created by a company to perform a function and is offered for use on websites and blogs. A widget is just a piece of code, called a "snippet," that is embedded in the HTML of a web page. Web designers and bloggers use widgets to make their sites more interesting and informative. For example, there are widgets that display daily weather forecasts, widgets that display slideshows of images, and widgets that can automatically organize blog posts by topic. Many are **intuitive** and change a website's appearance or potential functions according to inputs that both designers and users provide.

There are thousands upon thousands of widgets available. Some of them are called popups because they pop up a few seconds after the website loads. Some popular ones that you may have seen on websites include an invitation to chat with a customer service representative, a bar that lets people know the website uses cookies, and product reviews. Smartphones also have the ability to display widgets, such as showing the time and date on the home screen of the phone.

This makes it easy for a user to click on the page they are looking for instead of accidentally clicking on a different one.

A simple menu is easy to make, loads quickly, and works best for websites with no more than 16 pages. Dropdown navigation menus take up less space on the page and are more interesting, but they require extra coding to build. One way to make dynamic web pages is with a coding language called PHP. HTML is a language that is used to change the way the website appears to users. However, PHP is used to

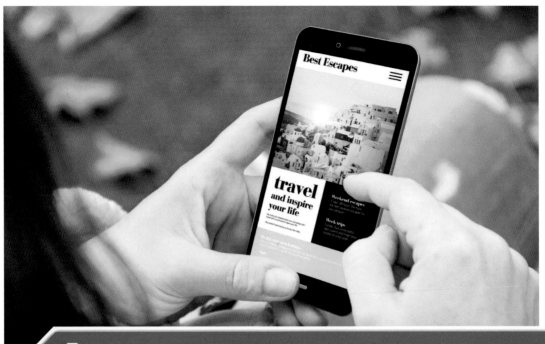

ON A MOBILE SITE, SAVING SPACE IS IMPORTANT SO THE SCREEN DOES NOT LOOK CLUTTERED AND CONFUSING. A DYNAMIC MENU THAT IS SYMBOLIZED BY THREE HORIZONTAL LINES IN THE CORNER CAN HELP WITH THIS.

communicate with servers. It takes information from the server and displays it on the website. PHP has become an increasingly common tool designers turn to when they want to make their website more interesting.

Think About It

1. What are some benefits and drawbacks to having a website that uses only HTML?
2. Take a look at your favorite website. What things do you think the CSS controls?
3. Why do we need multiple programming languages?

CHAPTER FOUR

GOING LIVE

O nce the website has been planned, designed, and coded, it is time to open it to the public. This is referred to as "going live" or "launching." There are a few things that need to be done to go live. These include getting a host and domain for the site as well as checking to make sure everything on the site works. This may sound like common sense, but after all the work to put the site together, sometimes people are so excited to go live that they forget to make sure all their links work. A website that does not work well will not impress the public.

DOMAINS AND HOSTS

A domain gives a person the right to use a particular **URL** for their site. The letters a URL ends with let users know the general purpose of the site. For example, .com and .net are used for commercial sites. These are the most common endings for a website and can cover anything from a person's bank to their recipe blog. Additionally, .org is used by nonprofit organizations, .gov is used by U.S. government organizations, and .edu is used by universities. Each country as well as some international organizations also have their own abbreviations that can be used. For example, some websites from the European Union end in .eu. These country-specific endings are more common in websites that are targeted at people who live within that country. For websites that want to attract international users, .com is more frequently used. Sometimes multiple endings can be grouped together. For example, a Canadian government website that has a similar name to an American government website might end with .gov.ca.

Domains are generally available through web-hosting services and cost a small amount of money per year. The name of the domain typically gives visitors an idea of what kind of website they are browsing, but an individual may choose any name for their website's domain as long as no one else already owns it. Sometimes a user who incorrectly enters a domain into their browser will be taken to a page that says the domain is available for purchase.

A web host is a service where the files that make up a website are stored. The host owns and manages the servers that serve the pages

A WEBSITE'S DOMAIN NAME IS IN ITS URL.

to visitors. It rents out server space to people who want to publish websites. After subscribing to a web-hosting service, people can upload the files that make up the website to the host's server when they want to publish the site. Most hosting services are inexpensive; for example, the most popular hosting site, Bluehost, starts at $2.95 per month as of early 2022. Wix and Squarespace act as both website builders and hosts, and each has a free option as well as a paid option. There are multiple different types of hosting websites. Each has its advantages and disadvantages, and some are better for certain purposes than others. Some of the most common include:

- **Shared hosting:** Many websites share a server, which keeps the cost down. Shared hosting is mostly used by individuals and small businesses. Many plans include important features such as an email address linked to the site. Although cheap and useful, traffic to other sites on the server can slow down an unrelated site. This is why it is preferred for websites that do not expect a lot of traffic.

- **Virtual private server (VPS) hosting:** For website owners that do not need their own server but want more storage space and customization options than a shared server can offer, this option is available. Each website is housed in a separate part of the server but still shares the server with other websites, so once again, the cost is kept low. Think of shared hosting as a dorm room that multiple students share, while VPS hosting is more like an apartment building. Websites that use VPS hosting have more storage space so they can handle more traffic, but they can still be affected by other websites on the server.

- **Dedicated server hosting:** If VPS is an apartment building, dedicated server hosting is a house. Instead of sharing space, a website owner hosts their site on their own server. This gives users much more control, but it is also much more expensive. Furthermore, running a dedicated server takes more skill; not everyone has the technical knowledge to do so. It is useful for large businesses or websites with a lot of traffic, such as Facebook.

- **Cloud hosting:** While most servers are physical computers that take up space in a room somewhere, cloud hosting allows people to host their website without the use of a server. Instead, the host is a network of multiple computers. This means multiple different servers work together, which is helpful for important websites such as the ones run by banks and government organizations. If one server goes down, it will not immediately cause the entire website to go down, so it will remain accessible to the people who need it.

FINISHING UP

Once the website is finished, a tool called a web **validator** is used to check for any inconsistencies with W3C standards. The validator looks at the HTML code and shows where any errors appear so they can easily be found and fixed.

After the site has been validated, it is ready to be published to the server. This is a matter of uploading the website files to the hosting service's computer. When the files have been uploaded, the site is live. Anyone who knows the URL can type it into their browser to visit the site. After some time—anywhere from four days to six months—search engines

WEB ANALYTICS AND SEO

Web analytics programs gather and analyze web usage data. Web analytics measure website traffic and serve as the basis for user analyses. There are two ways data is gathered. One is by logfile analysis, in which the web server's transactions are counted and analyzed. The second is by tagging, which records the number of times a page is loaded. Together, these measures help individuals and businesses make decisions about their websites. Such measures allow them to make changes that can drive traffic to the website. For example, they can analyze times of day with the most and least traffic and show ads on other websites at those times.

Search engine optimization (SEO) is also an important tool, especially for business websites. It refers to the process of driving traffic to a website from search engine results. People tend to only look at the first or second page of results, so being high on the list is very important. Having certain words in the search engine display, such as "bargain" and "how-to," also tends to increase the number of clicks on the page.

Analytics can show things such as how many people clicked on a website or ad.

such as Google add it to their **database**. Once this is done, people can also find the website without knowing the exact URL.

Once the site is published, it's time for one of the most important tasks: testing. Every page must be checked to make sure it is loading correctly. Every link on every page must also be tested to make sure they work properly and lead the user where they expect to go. When all of the pages and links check out, the website is finished.

KEEP IT WORKING

Most website designers choose to continually update their sites to keep visitors coming back for fresh content. Some webmasters place the date that new content appeared next to its link or headline. That way, visitors can see exactly when that content was added. It also helps to list updates or other content chronologically, or in order of the date they were added.

In addition to updating the website, testing is a big part of regular maintenance. Web pages and links should be tested periodically. Most importantly, the entire site should be retested any time it is updated. At these times, special attention should be paid to links to other websites, which sometimes change without notice.

Building and maintaining a website can be as easy or as challenging as a person wants it to be. It can be done with a deep knowledge of code or almost none at all. Not everyone needs a website, but in this age of technology, even a personal website can help connect people. A family might make a website to share personal news and photos with loved ones. A person who loves to cook may make a blog to share their recipes. An artist can create a website to share their paintings, photography, or other works with people around the world. The possibilities are endless once you know where to start.

A PERSONAL WEBSITE CAN ALLOW SOMEONE TO SHARE THEIR INTERESTS, TALENTS, AND KNOWLEDGE WITH THE REST OF THE WORLD OR JUST WITH THEIR FRIENDS AND FAMILY.

Think About It

1. What kind of website would you like to create?

2. Why do you think the W3C is necessary?

3. What happens to a website if it is not regularly maintained?

GLOSSARY

cache: A computer memory with very short access time used for storage of frequently or recently used instructions or data.

database: A collection of data that is organized especially to be used by a computer.

dynamic: Always active, energetic, or changing.

efficient: Able to bring about a desired result with little wasted time or energy.

embed: To insert something into a computer document.

hierarchy: A graded or ranked series.

intuitive: Allowing direct perception, by sense rather than by reason. In this context, the word describes a website that a visitor may use without having to make conscious decisions.

inventory: A supply of goods. Also, the list of such supplies.

novelty: Something new or unusual.

template: Something that serves as a pattern.

URL: Uniform resource locator; the address that lets a browser know exactly where on the web a site is located.

validate: To prove to be true, worthy, or justified.

FIND OUT MORE

BOOKS

Kurzius, Alexa. *Building a Website*. New York, NY: Children's Press, 2019.

McKinney, Donna Bowen. *Careers for Tech Girls in Graphic Design*. New York, NY: Rosen YA, 2019.

Taylor, Sam. *The Coding Workbook: Build a Website with HTML and CSS*. San Francisco, CA: No Starch Press, 2021.

WEBSITES

Code.org
code.org
Learn the basics of coding.

DoodleKit
www.doodlekit.com
This easy-to-use website builder for kids includes hundreds of free templates.

Envato Tuts+: Web Design for Kids
webdesign.tutsplus.com/series/web-design-for-kids--cms-823
This series of courses explains coding and visual design.

ORGANIZATIONS

American Institute of Graphic Arts (AIGA)
222 Broadway
New York, NY 10038
(212) 807-1990
www.aiga.org
Since 1914, this organization has been bringing graphic designers together as a community. AIGA also works to improve the public's understanding of the value of good design.

Black Girls CODE
1714 Franklin Street, Suite 100
San Francisco, CA 94162
(510) 398-0880
www.blackgirlscode.com
This organization works to give girls of color the skills and confidence to write their own code.

The Design Kids
humans@thedesignkids.org
thedesignkids.org
The Design Kids is a resource and community for students who are interested in pursuing a design career.

INDEX